Amazon

Fire Tablet

An Elaborate and Easy-to-Use Fire Tablet Guide

Table of Contents

Introduction

With the goal of reaching the expanded cloud of clients, most authors have produced eBooks that are doing around the internet. Other than just being educative, some content of the books is entertaining as well. However, these eBooks are protected, meaning that they are only available for reading on specific devices that support them.

eReaders have made accessing such books an easy endeavor than ever before. Amazon, for example, has produced several Kindle eReaders such as the Kindle Fire that are reliable for the users considering their unique characteristics that are appealing to the users.

The Kindle Fire comes with some great features that make it an excellent purchase from the market by Amazon. However, to get the best out of your investment, you have to understand all the features of the device as well as the procedures required for starting it up. The dealers accompany the device with the users' manual to make it easy for the user to enjoy his or her device.

This guidebook includes all the maintenance and safety information for the Kindle Fire tablet before paying for it. This also includes registering it with Amazon. This ensures that you see the value of your money and not regretting your hard-earned cash. The commonly asked questions and the steps involved in rectifying them are also included in this guidebook to impart vital knowledge about the product to act as the driving force towards acquiring the gadget.

Using the Kindle Fire for reading while on the go is only possible in case you have all the important information about the book at your fingertips. This will only be likely when you keenly go through the content of this guidebook, among the best of the guidebooks available in the market. Such easy-to-follow instructions make it easy to get the best out the electronic device. This has, since, attracted more users of this eReader globally and hence enhanced its market as a result.

Again, with the constant updating of the eReader, having the latest version of the users' guide will keep you on toes with the updates to make the product more competitive in the market by providing an enhanced and memorable experience to the users. There are many features that are hidden in this device that will only be unsurfaced when you go through this special guidebook with full concentration.

To be up to date with the current technology, therefore, consider purchasing this outstanding guide book from Amazon to get the best tricks and shortcut on using this Kindle Fire device. Create an account with Amazon, therefore, and be one of the sole beneficiaries of this special guidebook for the Kindle Fire lovers. Do not be the only one remaining on the bench while the others are on the move to enjoy the memorable experience of this Kindle Fire eReader in the ever evolving reading world.

Join the elites in identifying the simple tricks as well as the mind-bending features of this Kindle Fire device. With this, you qualify to be tagged "the best" provided you have a guidebook to walking you through the device properties and seeing the value of your money.

CHAPTER ONE: Getting to Know your Kindle Fire e-Reader

The Amazon Kindle Fire eReader is a version of the normal tablet that comes with a reasonable price tag. However, unlike the tablets, the Kindle eReader is for some reason the best option when it comes to reading the various eBooks purchased from Amazon. For example, the non-reflective electronic-ink displays, its light weight, and the significant, long-lasting battery life. This makes it reliable for regular reading.

Without getting technical, the Kindle Fire is a touchscreen device that is running on an Android operating system. This makes it easy to stream movies, downloading applications among other operations of the kind from the Amazon Kindle store.

To enjoy using this device. However, it is vital to understand all the features, including the information on how to set up your Kindle for easy navigation through the touchscreen in order to get the best out of it.

Identifying your Kindle model is an initial step in ensuring you get the best accessories and cases. Visit, therefore, the Amazon website to be sure you are using the updated tablet version (Kindle Fire).

Now that you have your Kindle Fire from Amazon, the first step involved is to register the device to your Amazo account. In case, however, you have purchased the gadget from the first buyer, then you need to replace the already-existing details with your own.

The Kindle Fire defining features

Just like mentioned earlier, Kindle Fire is a modified version of a tablet. There are, however, some hidden features that make it different.

Tap Notifications to read messages from the system or apps

Tap Quick Settings to adjust volume or brightness, manage Wi-Fi, and more

Tap here to switch between libraries or to shop for content

Swipe through the Carousel to view recent books, music, videos, websites, and apps, then tap to open an item

Pin your favorite content here by tapping and holding an item in the Carousel

Figure 1: Displaying features of the Kindle Fire

1. A Beautiful 7" IPS Display Screen

With the normal tablets like the iPad, a 10 HD screen is accepted as the standard screen size for a classic device. This Kindle Fire, however, prove that a 7" screen is the best when it comes to portability while keeping the price down as well. Other than the relatively smaller screen, this Kindle with a 7" screen is lighter, weighing less than a pound. The size is small enough to fit into your pocket as well as the purse.

This Fire HD 7 features a 1280x800 high definition Gorilla Glass display with over a million pixels (216 ppi). This provides a brighter and more enhanced display for vibrant colors at all angles. This is so because of the inclusive, innovative IPS (in-plane switching) technology and the advanced polarizing filter combination.

Just like the HD 6 and the HD 10, this HD 7 features a powerful quad-core processor, rear-facing cameras as well as the HD display.

Under glaring sunlight, it becomes difficult to read the content of your Kindle Fire. This is because it lacks an anti-glare property. The device is also made of a photophobic material that will melt in the direct sunlight above 10 degrees Celsius. However, it is possible to buy an anti-glare protector to help you continue enjoying the benefits of this device even when under a scorching sunlight. The screen, however, has a blue shade feature that tints the screen for night time use.

2. Music Player

In addition to the Kindle Fire including a speaker and headphone jack for listening to audio publications as well as using the text-to-text speech, this eReader can also be used as an MP3 player.

With this up-to-date eReader, you simply copy an MP3 file from your PC to the music folder on your device, using a USB cable.

Once you eject your Kindle from the computer, initiate the process by pressing the **Menu** button on the home screen then select the **Experimental**. From this Experimental page, a **Play Music** option appears next to the **Play MP3**. Enjoy your MP3s at your comfort once this is done.

To further make this interesting, it is possible to frequently pause or resume playback. This is made easy by simply pressing the **Alt+Space bar**. Skipping to the next song is also enhanced by simply pressing the **Alt+F**.

3. Picture Galleries

The Kindle Fire has the ability to support all the images in the JPEG, PNG as well as the GIF formats. It is, therefore, possible to store your images in your Kindle.

From your desktop using a USB cable, create a new folder named "picture" in the root directory. Include all your images in this folder (further create other subfolders if you desire).

Once this is done, disconnect the eReader from the computer and then press the **Alt+Z** in order to rescan the files on the Kindle's storage. Having done this, new options for each image gallery earlier created should appear in your library.

To color your experiencing of using this feature, Kindle Fire producers have included some relevant shortcuts and tricks.

f – toggle the full-screen mode

q – zooming in

w – zooming out

e – default zoom

c – returning to the actual image size

r – rotating the image

4. A Built-In Camera

The Kindle Fire HD has a built-in camera. This camera, however, is meant solely for use as a webcam with Skype app. That is, it is not for taking photos.

However, it is possible to unlock the camera by installing an app like the Photo Editor. This can be downloaded from the Amazon Appstore. This Photo Editor enables you to edit and afterward share the photos taken by the front-facing camera of this Kindle.

5. Wi-Fi Antenna, 4G Access

With the many Amazon produced eReaders, the Kindle Fire brags of a new antenna design supposed to create faster connections with fewer dropped signals. With this feature, it is possible to download books among other content to be read offline.

The outstanding speed of this antenna with the 4G access capability cannot be noticed unless when you are streaming the media.

Unfortunately, this 4G data plan has to be paid for on top of the price of the tablet.

6. Silk Browser

In this Kindle Fire, Amazon introduces a new Web browser. The Silk Web browser makes it easy for the tablet to display the websites by allowing the Amazon's servers pre-crunch the sites. This browser is important for Google searches because this tablet lacks Google as well as the Google Play.

However, using this Silk you cannot download the Chrome, Google maps or even sync your bookmarks between the devices.

7. Android Operation System

Unlike the earlier Kindle readers that ran on modified version of Linux, this new Kindle Fire runs on an Android (google's free Linux-based mobile operating system).

This highly modified version of Android is greatly controlled by buying things from the *Amazon.com*.

8. Immersion Reading Feature

This unique feature enables the user to simultaneously hear the audio and read the contents of the eBooks while the texts are highlighted. This characteristic is advantageous to those users with specific conditions such as dyslexia among other reading disabilities.

What one unique fact about this read aloud features is that the publisher can disable when they feel that their customer would not buy the audio books, listening to the robotic voice. This is unlike the other eReaders with this property.

9. The X-Ray Feature for the Books and Movies

With this feature, the user is able to access all the relevant information. Such as the dictionary entries for books, IMDB information for movies and the Wikipedia among other Web information relevant to the content of the publication such as the movies.

10. Parental Controls Feature

With the interesting and adventurous games, parents hand their children this shopping device assuming the associated consequences. This Kindle Fire, therefore, introduces the new parental controls that are aimed at preventing the unintended purchases. Other than for shopping, this feature limits both the games and video time in favor of reading time.

11. Whispersync Feature for Audio Books

Nearly all the Kindle Fire devices, including the Kindle Fire, include a **whispersync for an audio** feature that enables the user to sync between devices. this remains handy when you are using the two different devices (one in your living room and the other in your car, for example).

12. The Menus, Icons, and Gestures

Unlike the many Android devices available, the Kindle Fire has a **Home** button that is ubiquitous and found in the lower-left corner of the gadget.

The **Settings menu** is opened by pressing the appropriate cog-like icon found in the top-right of the display. This Settings page has options to toggle the rotation lock, enhances the display brightness, connect to Wi-Fi, syncing books with Amazon, adjusting the volume as well as accessing the host of advanced settings.

However, recent studies indicate that the **Home** button and the **Back** button (located in the middle of the bottom edge of the device display) are the most commonly used. This gadget, therefore, includes an app-specific context menu as well as the **Search** button to enable the users easily access the respective buttons.

Just like any other touch-sensitive device, a variety of gestures enables one to essentially interact with his or her Kindle Fire with the most convenience. To begin with, the basic tablet version of a left-mouse click on a computer offers a context menu with additional option scenarios. The swipe option, for example, will enable you to browse the contents of your device. This is particularly important when it comes to Newsstand view as well as browsing.

A **pitch-to-zoom gesture** using the forefinger and the thumb is helpful when it comes to zooming in and out of the images as well as the web pages.

Across the top of the gadget, a narrow bar displays your registered name, time and other information like the battery life and the wireless connectivity. Information about the new emails, apps among the many other important features are found in this notification area. The notifications are displayed as a number in a gray disc. Tapping this disc to expand and view, will help you get to the appropriate app you desire at that particular time.

Once you are done checking the notifications, click the **Clear All** button and the **Home**.

In addition to this information, tapping the button on the lower edge of the tablet will wake your Kindle Fire from sleep mode. This same button is the one used to power on and off the gadget. In case your device goes to a lock screen after a period of inactivity, however, swipe from right to left across the characteristic yellow band with an arrow that displays on the screen. This helps the user to go back to the **Home screen**.

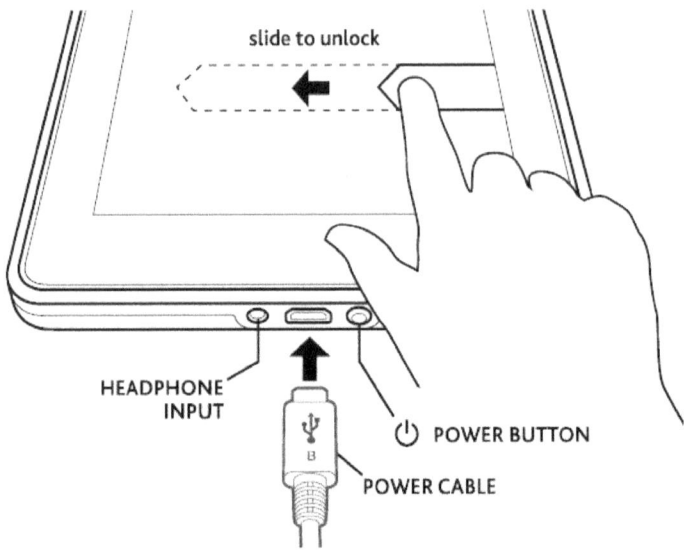

Figure 2: the Kindle Fire Hardware and the yellow
band for unlocking the Kindle

13. The Carousel feature

The users would desire to revisit the web pages,
newspapers, videos, music and other recently
accessed publications. The Kindle Fire, however,
ensures that these recently accessed documents are
added to the Carousel for a future revisit.

To advance through this feature, swipe your finger to
view the items arranged in chronological order, with
the most recent appearing first. Press and hold on the
item you desire. This displays the contextual menu,

including the **Add to Favorite**, **Remove from Carousel**, and **Remove from Device**.

14. Favorites

In order to add a book, magazine, video, an app or even an album to the Favorite, press and hold on the item you need to display the contextual menu, then select the **Add to Favorites**.

To remove an item from the Favorite, however, press and hold on the item to display the contextual menu, and then select the **Remove from Favorites**.

CHAPTER TWO: Getting Started with your Kindle Fire

Once you have unpacked your Kindle Fire, you may need to charge it while setting it up. Just like any other Amazon Kindle, this Fire comes with its own USB cable and a power adapter. Plug the smaller end of the cable into your Kindle Fire, while the other end into a computer. Using the adapter. However, the user can as well plug the Kindle into a regular wall socket for quick charging.

1. Switching the Kindle Fire on

In case your Kindle has enough power to start, turn it on by pressing the small circular button located at the bottom of your device (refer to figure 2). Having powered your Kindle on for the first time displays a series of screens that guides you in setting up and registering your gadget. Follow, therefore, the onscreen instructions in order to help you establish any connection and finish the both the setup and the registration process.

However, after about five minutes of inactivity, your Kindle's screen will go dark. This is known as either the "sleep" or the "standby" mode. This feature helps in conservation of battery life of this tablet. When it is on, and you tap the power button, your gadget will go to "sleep." To wake the device, however, simply press the power button. Once it is awakened, it will show new background images or the ad, depending on your device setting status. This acts as an easy way of cycling through the images in your gadget.

It is possible to set how long the device takes before it goes to "sleep" if not used. To do this, select the **Settings** then the **Display & Sounds** section.

Some covers for the Kindle Fire includes a built-in auto-sleep on/off feature. Once the cover is closed, it automatically puts the tablet to "sleep, " and when opened, it automatically "wakes up."

It is also important to note that by pressing and holding the power button, turns the power off. An option to **Power off** or **Cancel** will pop up. Simply tap the **Power off** button, and your tablet will turn off.

2. Connect to a Wi-Fi network

Before enjoying any good that comes with this device, a stable and reliable connection is mandatory. You can, therefore, connect to a Wi-Fi network by simply tapping the **Quick Settings** icon located at the top of the screen, then choose the Wi-Fi.

From a list of available networks scanned, select your network of choice and enter the password if any in order to begin enjoying your eReader. Your Kindle Fire can as well recognize the available networks with the help of a WPS compatible router. This is enabled by first selecting the **wireless network** of your own choice, and then pressing the **WPS** button on your router. To display the strength of your network signal via the indicator, select the WPS again. This Wi-Fi connection procedure is similar when one desires to use a public hotspot.

With its built-in cellular 4G connection, the connection is relatively faster compared to that of the other Kindles. To further improve the device connectivity. However, some users prefer to add their personal network (either hotspot or Wi-Fi).

In case you have problems setting up a Wi-Fi at your home, contact your Internet Service Provider (ISP).

Once you have a reliable connection, proceed with the registration process.

3. Registering your Kindle Fire to Amazon

Once you turn on your Kindle after unpacking your Kindle Fire, you will either be required to register it to your Amazon account or confirm the registration in case you get it when already preregistered. To finish this registration, therefore, follow the promptings from that appear on the screen during the process.

In case you don't have an Amazon account, click the **New to Amazon?**. This leads to a link that takes you to the **Create an Amazon Account** screen, with fields where you are required to feed in your name, personal email address, and the password. Retype the password for confirmation. Once you have filled all the fields, tap the **Continue** icon once you have all the information keyed in.

To register your Kindle Fire, enter your Amazon account information, the email address and then the password in the appropriate fields. It is advisable to deselect the Show Password check box to protect your password from the meddling eyes surrounding you.

Once all the information is entered, tap the **By Registering, You Agree to All of the Terms Found**

Here link in case you need to read the terms and conditions.

Now aware of the terms, tap the **Close** button to return to the registration screen. Tap, next, the **Register** button to complete the registration process with a new or existing Amazon account.

Select your time zone from the list displayed on your screen. Once you have selected your zone from the list, click the **Back** button located in the bottom-left corner. This returns you to the **Time Zone screen**.

A final screen appears reminding you to confirm your account. Do this by simply clicking the **Continue** button. If for some reasons you have entered your account information incorrectly, tap the **Not <Your Name>** link to correct your account information then return to this screen and complete the registration process.

The next screen that is labeled **Connect Social Networks** indicate the social networks you are connected to. If there are some labeled accounts displaying on your Kindles screen, as a result of the connections you may have to your Amazon account, such as **Connect Your Twitter Account**, tap them to connect.

At this point now, several screens acquaint you with the Kindle Fire HD features and a guideline on how to use the major ones. To proceed with a brief tutorial, tap the **Next** button that is located on the middle-right side of the screens.

When you are done, tap the **Close** button to go to the Kindle Fire HD **Home screen**.

4. Shopping for the Titles

Amazon includes a selection of videos, music, applications, TV shows, newspapers, and eBooks among other useful content for your Kindle Fire. To access these important content, click the **Store** link in the top right corner of any **Content library**. To go back to the Content library, tap the **Library**. Within the store, browse the titles by categories, checking the best sellers, while as well viewing the recommendations.

The presence of movie trailers, song previews, as well as the free book samples provides a risk-free trial before you opt to buy the content for your Kindle.

Any title you select would be directly delivered to your Kindle in the presence of an active Wi-Fi connection. This has an advantage in that you are able to access a publication before it is even available in print for others without this device to have access to them. When the connection is not active, any new subscription issue will become available once your Wi-Fi network is active.

When you desire to shop other products from Amazon, click the **Apps** on the Home screen, then choose the **Amazon Shop app** to browse the item you need to purchase.

However, to manage your Amazon account, simply click the **1-Click account**, then the **Wish List and more**, click, next, the **Menu** icon found on the **Options** bar.

For the easy purchasing of the different content for your device, it is important to first set up a payment method. To do this, visit the **Manage your Kindle page** using your web browser. From the Home Screen, open the **Home Menu**, then select the **Experimental**. Just like all the other Kindles, this Fire uses the Amazon's 1-click Payment method for easy purchasing of the Kindles' content of their users' choices. With this method, those with an Amazon account can consider using either the debit or credit card with their default shipping address indicated in their Amazon account.

To customize your payment option, however, click your **1-Click Payment method**, then press **Edit**. From here, either select or rather add a new debit or credit card for the 1-Click Payment. Click, finally, the **Continue** icon to confirm that the changes are saved.

5. Safeguarding your Kindle contents

Parental Control feature protects the Kindle from access from unauthorized users (such as the children) who would by mistake purchase contents from the Amazon, or sometimes delete the important content from the Kindle library.

Setting up a password is another measure to ensure no one is able to access the content of your Kindle without your knowledge. Setting up this security code is an easy-to-follow step: press the **Home**, followed by the **Menu** icon. From this Menu page, select **Settings**, then scroll down to the option **Device Password**. Click this tab then select the **Turn on the** icon. Type a password of your choice. Assigning a password hint is relatively important in ensuring you do not forget the password set.

To complete this setup, tap the **Submit** icon in order to confirm the passcode. This as well puts your device's content safe from invaders.

6. The Kindle FreeTime App

For children below the age of 9 years, installing a Kindle FreeTime application will be helpful in sieving the content they access. That is, it controls the videos, music, books and apps your child will have access to. This application has its own carousel as well as the media sections for every profile you create.

The application comes with a bright blue background to help you instantly know that the app is in use. This makes it easy for you to monitor your child in case they are accessing the out of bound content.

✓ Creating a Kindle FreeTime App

Once you open a Kindle FreeTime app, you are required to either create and confirm a password or enter one in case you have it. You can enter Parental Control password.

After entering the password, create a profile for your child. This is done by tapping the **Manage Child Profiles** and then **Add New Profile**. This is done in case you are not prompted to create the profile upon entering and confirming your set password.

From the display, tap the **Tap to set photo** in order to include a profile icon of your child's choice if not his or her own photo.

The next step involves tapping the **text box** in order to enter your child's first name. Your can optionally add the child's birthday to help you set different security features for him or her. Select, next, the **sex of the child**. That is whether male or female. If the book is for children with mixed sexes, you can skip this part. Once this is done, click the **Next** icon that appears to see a new profile added to the list of **Child Profiles**.

Guided by the Child Profile, tap the **Manage Your Content** to approve the content for your child to the **Child Profile** from the **All Kids apps** in your cloud. Once you have selected the content for your child or children, tap the **Done** button at the top right of your screen display.

Once the profile is complete, you can select the **Edit Child Detail** option to edit the data including the image, name, birthday, among other information.

CHAPTER THREE: The Kindle Fire Content

Regardless of the small size of your Kindle Fire tablet that makes it convenient to carry along, the gadget has an internal memory of up to 8GB and an additional external disc slot for storage of your content. With this device, therefore, users are able to read their books, play games, listen to music, watch their stored videos among other content while offline, provided you toggle to the Cloud and download the content to your device.

1. Finding content for your Kindle Fire

The Amazon's Kindle Store provides access to a selection of reading content for your device. At discounted prices, you can acquire any book, video, music, and any other content you wish to add to your Kindle. Luckily enough, it is a great experience to read the periodicals on your Kindle due to the Kindle Fire's full-color characteristic.

Being that this Kindle Fire is a product of Amazon, sourcing of its content does not limit to Amazon. You can find books and other content from either your local library, borrowing from friends, or even download them from other online stores and websites before transferring them to your Kindle Fire. By the help of the OverDrive app, it is possible to transfer the content from your local store into your Kindle.

Amazon provides a risk-free taste of its content for your Kindle. Once you like the content, an option to either borrow or purchase it will appear. However, in case it is not available for borrowing, the **Borrow for Free** button won't be visible. In addition to this, if you had borrowed a book a month earlier, this **Borrow for the Free** button is grayed.

The either bought or borrowed Kindle content from the Kindle Store displays on the **Books screen** as well as in the **Carousel** located on the Home screen.

2. Content Libraries

All your downloaded content are stored in the Kindle Fire libraries, including the content stored by Amazon in the Cloud. These libraries include the following Newsstand, Books, Videos, Apps among several others. Other than the **Docs library** (where documents that you receive from your device via the e-mail, or sideloaded from the computer are placed), however, these libraries offer has a **Store** button that allows the users to browse and buy more content by simply tapping the button.

For easy access to these content libraries, an **Options bar** is located at the bottom of each Content library screen. These options vary depending on the content type. However, there are some standard options that are included at the bottom of each content library:

- ❖ **Home**: from anywhere on your Kindle Fire, this icon returns you to the Home screen.
- ❖ **Menu**: click on this Menu icon in order to view additional options that are related to the content type you have selected.
- ❖ **Back**: this icon helps the user to retrace his or her steps when accessing the   Kindle content.
- ❖ **Share**: considering this icon enables the user to share his or her thoughts with other readers.
- ❖ **Search**: this option is useful when trying to search your preferred Content library.

When some applications are running, the Options bar may be hidden.

Figure 3: Icon showing the hidden Options bar

This can be expanded either by simply tapping the arrow displayed at the bottom of the screen or by swiping from the bottom of the device.

When utilizing your Kindle content, a simple tap at the middle of the screen displays the Options bar for further experiences.

Tapping the device while in a library such as the Music library displays only the content you have downloaded. However, tapping the Cloud tab shows you all the content, including all the purchases and the free content that are stored in the Amazon Cloud library.

3. Managing the Kindle Fire content

To get the best out of your Kindle Fire, the user must possess the knowledge on how to manage the content of their eReader. Understanding how to avoid the accidental deletion of the Kindle content, for example, is vital when you need to see the value of your hard-earned cash. This chapter, therefore, provides all the information that would prove to be useful to the new users for the proper management of their Kindle content in their quest of getting the best out of this outstanding eReader.

With a registered Kindle Fire, tap on the **Manage Your Kindle Content and Devices** located at the top of the screen display. To specifically manage the content of the content library, select the **Your Content** from among the three options that would appear: **Your Content**, **Your Devices,** and the **Settings**. From this point, one can either decide to deliver content to their Kindle or delete it.

a) Transferring content to your Kindle Fire

Just like any other Amazon Kindle, select the titles that you desire to deliver into your tablet from the Kindle store. **Check** the box next to your selected headings and then conclude by tapping the **Deliver** icon. A list of the connected devices would appear. Select, therefore, from the list the gadget you would wish to send your content. Again click the **Deliver** button to complete the content transfer.

However, to transfer the content from the computer to your Kindle Fire, the following is a systematic procedure that facilitates this operation:

- First, connect your Kindle Fire to your PC using a USB cable.
- Once your device is connected to the PC or laptop, unlock your device
- From the PC, your Kindle will appear as an external storage drive or volume on the computer desktop.
- Drag and drop the items you desire to transfer from your computer to the Kindle into the applicable or customized folders.
- Once the transfers are complete, tap the Disconnect option located at the bottom of the Kindle Fire screen and eject it from the PC. Unplug, therefore, the USB cable.

b) **Deleting items either from your Fire or your Amazon Cloud**

❖ **Removing items from your Fire**

To delete a downloaded content from your device, without necessarily deleting it entirely from your personal Amazon account for downloading at a later date. Press and hold an item on the Device screen in order to display its contextual menu. From the pop-up menu, select the **Remove from Device**.

❖ **Removing item from the carousel**

However, if the content is located in the carousel, simply long-tap the item you have selected for management and the choose the **Remove from Carousel** from the pop-up menu.

❖ **Removing the items from the Amazon Cloud**

In case you need to remove the item from your Amazon Cloud for reasons like de-cluttering your device's Cloud screens using your Kindle, follow the following systematic procedure:

➢ Visit the apps from the **Cloud menu** on your Kindle Fire
➢ From the Cloud, press and hold the app you desire to delete for about three seconds until a

pop-up menu appears. A brief tap would start downloading the application to your device.

➢ On the pop-up menu, complete the removal of the selected item by clicking the **Delete from Cloud**. Press the **OK** icon to confirm the process once prompted.

CHAPTER FOUR: The Kindle Fire Settings

To enhance your experience of using the Kindle Fire, this guidebook provides the settings procedure in each and every chapter. In this section, however, specific Quick settings options are explained in details for the new users to be familiar with some of these general settings.

Located on the **Status bar** is a **Quick Settings** icon that displays settings for the most commonly performed tasks as well as the volume control.

Figure 4: a status bar with the commonly used display settings

A. Locking and unlocking the screen orientation

The Kindle Fire features an accelerometer that can sense the orientation of this gadget. That is, the device's screen will automatically rotate to match the orientation of the device when you are holding it.

When reading a web page in a portrait mode, for example, you might need to prevent the automated screen rotation. This is done by following a systematic procedure:

- ❖ With the screen displaying the anticipated alignment, swipe the Status bar down in order to open the general settings drawer.
- ❖ Tap the **Unlocked** option to lock the orientation. When this is done, the label on the icon will change to **Locked**.

The same applies when you need to unlock the orientation. That is, tap the **Locked** icon on the Status bar.

B. Volume adjustment

A toggle button on the Status bar allows you to adjust the volume of your Kindle. A volume meter appears on the screen indicating the volume level. To do this follow the following procedure:

- ❖ Swipe the **Status button** in order to open the Settings drawer
- ❖ Click the **Volume** icon. This will, as a result, display a volume control
- ❖ Slide, then, the volume control towards the right to increase the volume, and to the left to decrease the volume.

In a portrait mode, however, this is not the case. If you press the button to the right, the volume decreases. When you swipe to the left, the volume increases.

Observe, therefore, your volume control while using these buttons to adjust the volume to your liking.

It is also possible to adjust the volume directly on the screen.

C. Screen brightness adjustment

The Kindle Fire requires that you brighten the screen for a better view of the displayed content. This consumes more power than any other device available. It, however, comes with an icon that allows the user to adjust the brightness of the display depending on the ambient light:

- ❖ Swipe the Status bar down in order to open the Settings drawer
- ❖ Click on the **Brightness** option
- ❖ Slide the brightness control, therefore, to the right to increase the brightness and to the left to decrease the brightness.

D. Connect to Wi-Fi

A reliable network connection is vital for a memorable experience with your Kindle Fire. From the Settings drawer, select the **Wi-Fi** option. Tap the **On** option next to **Wi-Fi** and select from a list of detectable Wi-Fi networks by tapping the **Connect** tab.

When connecting to a network, confirm that **Airplane Mode** is **Off**.

When not in use, it is important to turn off the Wi-Fi in order to minimize the power utilization by the device.

- ❖ Swipe the Status bar down to open the Settings drawer
- ❖ Click on the **Wi-Fi**
- ❖ Tap **Off** next to the **Wi-Fi** icon to turn off the Wi-Fi.

E. Syncing the device

This Sync icon is helpful for users desiring to sync their device with their cloud content. For this to function, there must be a network connection.

By tapping this icon, you manually initiate the downloading of new content or continue the downloads that were interrupted.

- ❖ Swipe the Status bar down to open the Settings drawer
- ❖ Tap on the **Sync** to sync your gadget.

F. Checking the device information among other additional settings

Other than the explained setting options above, tapping the More icon displays information about your Kindle Fire.

- ❖ Swipe the status bar down to open the Settings drawer
- ❖ Tap the More. From this point, all the information you require about the device, including the **My Account**, **Help & Feedback**, **the Parental Controls**, **Security**, **Display,** and **Sounds** among much other information.

CHAPTER FIVE: Maintenance Information for your Kindle Fire

To enjoy the benefits of this Kindle Fire, this user guide provides all the information that guide the new users. This chapter, however, provides the safety information that must be considered before opting to use the device. The information contained in this here also help in the maintenance of your Kindle Fire.

Read, therefore, all the instructions to maintain your device to last long and as well avoid the adverse effects of fire, injuries, damage, and electric shock:

1. Servicing the Kindle

To get the best out of the Kindle Fire, regular servicing is mandatory. Contact, therefore, the Amazon Customer Support whose contact details are found at www.amazon.com/kindlesupport.

In the case of the Kindle Fire defection in materials and workmanship under the ordinary consumer use within the one-year limited warranty period, Amazon will, as permitted by law, service your device. However, faulty service may void the warranty.

2. Handling the glass parts

The outside cover of the Kindle Fire is made of glass. In the case of any breakage, chipping, or cracking of the glass, terminate the usage of the device and avoid touching or attempting to remove the damaged glass.

Contact Amazon to help in either repairing or replacing the gadget. In case it is still within the limited warranty period, no payment will be made.

3. Battery safety

Unlike the other Amazon Kindles, the Fire has a battery with a relatively shorter life. This rechargeable battery must only be charged under the temperature ranging from 0 to 35 degrees Celcius.

In the case of the need to replace this battery in your Kindle Fire, an authorized service provider is the best. For more information about the batteries, however, visit the www.amazon.com/kindleterms.

4. Avoid using the Kindle Fire around other electronic devices

Considering the technology used in manufacturing it, the Kindle Fire generates, uses and can as well radiate radio frequency energy if the user assumes the safety instructions.

This ignorance can affect the radio communications and the electronic equipment. The external radio frequency signals affect the inadequately shielded or improperly installed entertainment systems, electronic operating system and the personal medical devices (hearing aids, pacemakers).

Make sure to consult the manufacturers of this electronic equipment on whether their product is shielded against the external radio frequencies.

5. Wireless safety and compliance

In specific areas where you are not allowed to use the wireless service with the fear that it would cause danger or interference, turn off your wireless connection.

In air transport, for example, turning on the wireless connection produces the radio-frequency energy that interferes with the aircraft systems. To curb this, however, aviation agencies such as the United States Federal Aviation Administration Regulations advice that anyone boarding an airplane should consider using their devices' wireless services.

6. Avoid using your Kindle Fire or its accessories in wet conditions

Be careful to avoid wetting your Kindle Fire. For example, do not use your device when it is raining, or near a sink. In addition to this, do not use the Kindle Fire when eating to avoid spilling food or liquid in your device.

In case it gets wet, unfortunately, unplug all the cables and turn off the wireless. This will force the screen revert to the screen saver. Avoid turning on the device until the device dries completely.

Do not, however, dry your Kindle Fire using the external heat sources like the microwave.

7. Cleaning your Kindle Fire

For some mismanagement issues, the screen might become dirty. Because of this, however, manufacturers and the long-term users advise that a clean screen enhances the aesthetic value of your Kindle Fire.

Clean, therefore, the screen with a soft, clean clothing. Wiping the screen using a material with an abrasive property will lower its quality by introducing scratches on the screen.

8. Purchase a Kindle Fire cover

Amazon produces covers for the Kindle Fire, with built-in auto-sleep on/off features. This ensures that the device goes to sleep once it is covered. This, as a result, minimizes the energy usage by the Kindle.

These covers also ensure that the screens are safeguarded against scratches.

9. Other maintenance procedure

Avoid exposing your Kindle Fire to the extreme cold or heat. For example, do place it in a freezer with extremely cold temperature or next to the oven producing extremely hot conditions.

CHAPTER SIX: Common Problems with Amazon Kindle Fire and strategies to fix them

The Kindle Fire is, according to many folks, an Amazon stand-up device. This device running a custom version of Android has seen numerous upgrades. This HD that comes in various sizes has decent specs regardless of its relatively low price.

Unfortunately, even the most popular products have some downsides. The Kindle Fire is not an exception. The long-term users have reported a number of problems that have for a long time undermined the marketing of this product. In this chapter, therefore, some common problems and the recommended strategies to fix them.

A. Problem starting up the Kindle Fire

Quite a number of the Kindle Fire users report that their devices fail to open up properly. This can go as far as the logo then it gets stuck.

In this state, your device won't be recognized by the computer when plugged in.

Solution

- If this is the case, rebooting the device can help in clearing out the glitches that are responsible for causing the problem. This entails holding the power button for about twenty seconds. Once it goes off, press the power button to enjoy your Kindle.

- In case you think the battery is empty, plug your Kindle for about 20 minutes. Press and hold, therefore, the power button for about 40 seconds until it restarts.

- Getting into the recovery menu is also a way of curbing this problem. To do this, turn off your Kindle then hold the Power and the Volume down buttons simultaneously. Once on the recovery menu, use the Volume keys to highlight the options and the Power button to select them.

- A factory reset can be considered as well though it wipes all data in your device.

B. Your Kindle not connecting to a PC

While trying to move files into their Kindle Fires from the computer via a USB cable, your Kindle might fail to indicate on the computer screen or a message that the device is disconnected or not responding.

Solutions

- Turn off both your device and the computer for few seconds before turning them on again. This is believed to reset both the Kindle Fire and the computer.
- Consider using another USB cable, in case the problem is in that.
- Try a different USB port in case your PC has other ports.
- Try to perform a hard reset. This is done by holding the power button for about 30 seconds, assuming all prompts on the device, until it goes off. Restart the gadget once again and observe the problem once again.
- Confirm that your Kindle Fire drivers are up-to-date and that they are functioning well. In case this is the issue, download new drivers specifying your device. This is done by googling the **Kindle Fire Drivers**.

- Factory reset your Kindle
- Right-click on the device in the Device Manager then choose the Uninstall to remove it from the computer. Plug it out then plug it back to enable the windows to reinstall your gadget properly.
- If the problem persists, consider the cloud storage services like the Dropbox, Mega or the Google Drive to get the files onto your Kindle Fire.

C. Internal errors

When using your device, you might encounter an error message saying "*An internal error occurred.*" In the case of lack of network connectivity, a notification "*This can be caused by lack of network connectivity.*" It is, therefore, mandatory you have a good and reliable network connection.

Solution

- Force the application to stop. To do this,
    - Swipe down from top to display the status bar

- From the more icon, select the **Manage Applications**
- Tap, then, the **Installed Applications** and then locate the app that is   misbehaving
- Click on the app and then tap the **Force Stop** prompt.

+ Consider trying a hard reset
+ Clear the application data. To do this, follow the first five steps involved in the forcing the application to stop. In the last step, however, tap the **Clear Data** option.
+ Deregister and then re-register your Kindle Fire
+ Confirm that the date is set correctly
+ Try all the troubleshooting procedures for a failed Wi-Fi connection.

D. Screen flicker

Sometimes visible fading between cycles appear on the screen display. This screen flicker appears either periodically, in specific applications, or a constant issue in some devices.

Solution

- Turning off the auto brightness.
- Consider a hard reset

E. Overheating

With the current tablets, overheating is a constant experience when performing resource intensive operations.

Solution

- Contact the Amazon Customer Support

F. Charging problems

The fact that your device is not charging is an issue. Some devices refuse to charge, charge slowly, while others will charge only a fraction.

Solution

- Shut it down then charge it for the next couple of hour before turning it on
- Replace a USB cable that is not working in case it is the one with the problem

G. Misbehaving keyboard

Sometimes the touch screen keyboards can decide to revolt.

Solution

- Clean your screen, in case the filthy status of the screen is responsible for the discouraging experience. Do this with a clean and soft cloth
- Reset your Amazon Kindle Fire
- Factory reset your Kindle Fire

H. Pre-installed browser will not start

This Kindle comes with a built-in Silk browser that has been criticized for its slow performance as well as constant crashing. Sometimes this browser fails to start completely.

Solution

- Consider rebooting your device by holding the power button for about 20 seconds and the turning it on once again.
- Clear all the data on the Silk browser. This is done by going to **Settings**>**Applications**> **Manage all applications**> **All applications**> **Silk browser**> **Clear data**.

- Try to download an alternative browser like the *Dolphin browser*.

I. Email not working

Sometimes it is possible for your email accounts to fail to work on your Kindle Fire HD.

Solution

- Download a third party e-mail app to replace the installed one.

Not limited to the problems mentioned above, there are several others that different users have reported about this Kindle Fire. Amazon has been utilizing the reviews by the product's users to identify these issues and updating on the means of rectifying the technicality. Contact the Amazon Customer Support for further clarification on managing nearly all the problems with this Kindle Fire tablet.

CHAPTER SEVEN: Conclusion

First of all, I would like to thank you for considering going through this Kindle Fire tablet guidebook. This is an amazing motivator for the new users of this device.

Understanding all the features of this Kindle Fire provides the users with a clue on how to handle the gadget and get the best out of it, as a result.

Registering your Kindle Fire to your Amazon account is the initial step involved in enjoying the memorable experience that comes with this device. Once you registered, you can switch your device and browse through the various content libraries for the best experience ever. All these, however, are possible provided the Kindle Fire is connected to a reliable network. In case, however, you have a device registered to someone else's account, you are required to deregister that account and then re-register it to your own account.

Managing the Kindle Fire library is mandatory to enhance your experience. That is, either adding the new content to your Kindle or deleting the content you no longer need.

Maintaining your Kindle Fire in a good state will ensure yo enjoy the benefits that come along with it for many days to come. These instructions, as well, safeguards your health as the user.

Considering the regular review on Amazon products, there are a number of problems that are experienced by the global users of this Kindle. Amazon has taken the initiative of providing the information on how to surpass these problems.

Go, therefore, into the market and acquire this modern Kindle Fire tablet for an enhanced and memorable experience.

Finally, if you enjoyed this book, please take the time to share your thoughts and post a review on Amazon. It would be greatly appreciated! Thank you and good luck!

www.ingramcontent.com/pod-product-compliance
Lightning Source LLC
Chambersburg PA
CBHW060105300526
45788CB00015B/1609